Hello!
I am a wolf.

I0108781

Wolves are excellent hunters and can run up to speeds of 35 miles (56 km) per hour.

Wolves have incredible stamina. They can cover anywhere between 10 to 30 miles (16 to 48 km) in a day.

Wolves come in different colors, including gray, black, white, and even reddish-brown.

Wolf fur has two layers. The outside layer is long and tough. The layer underneath is soft and fluffy.

My super special fur keeps me warm and cozy.

Wolf paws are like dog paws, but have a thicker pad on the bottom that helps them hunt.

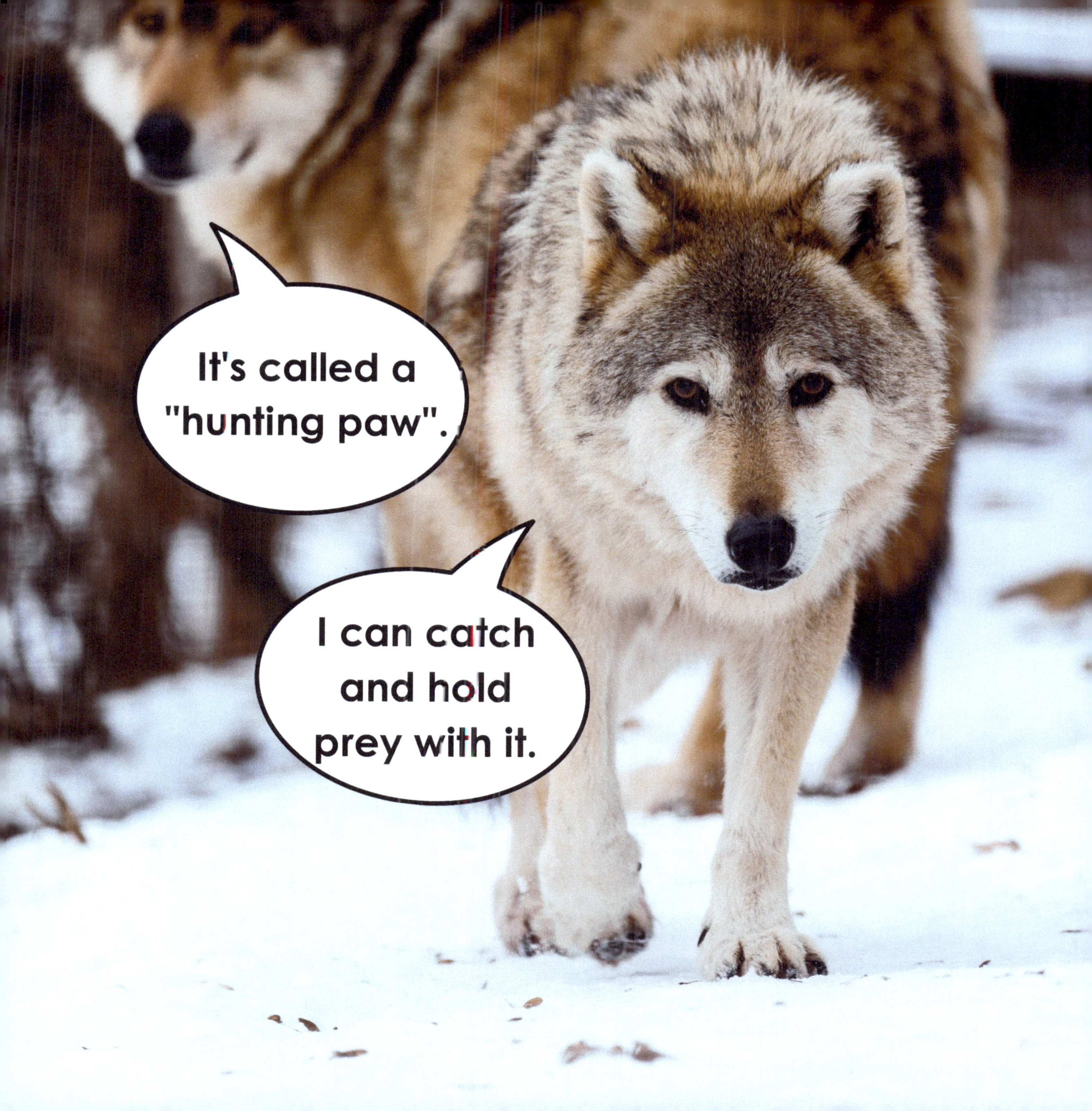
It's called a "hunting paw".
I can catch and hold prey with it.

A group of wolves is called a "pack".

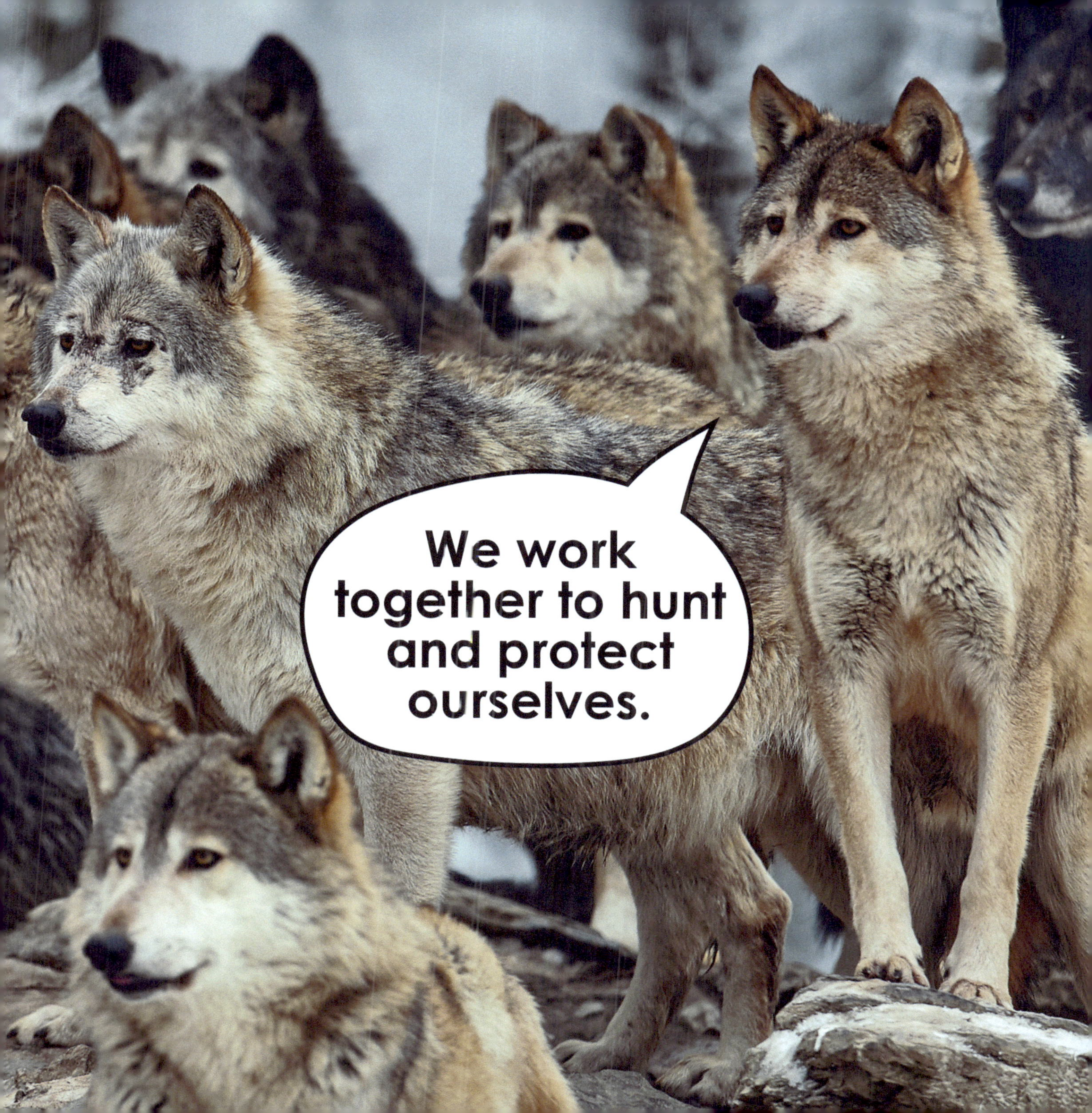
We work together to hunt and protect ourselves.

Every pack has an alpha pair. They are the strongest male and female in the pack.

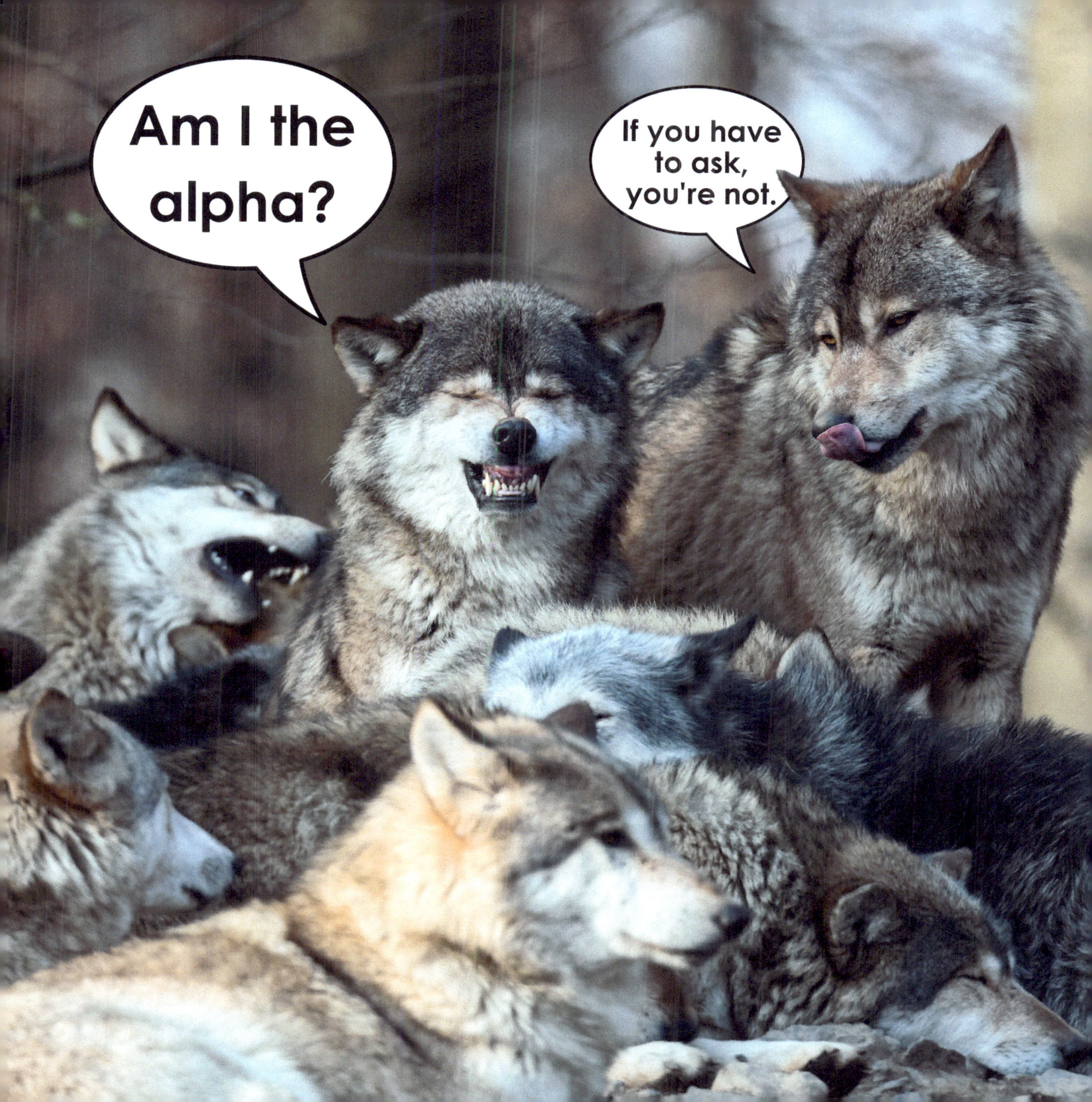
Am I the alpha?
If you have to ask, you're not.

Wolves communicate with each other using howls, barks, and body language.

Let's get some lunch.

Wolves howl to communicate with their pack and warn other packs to stay away.

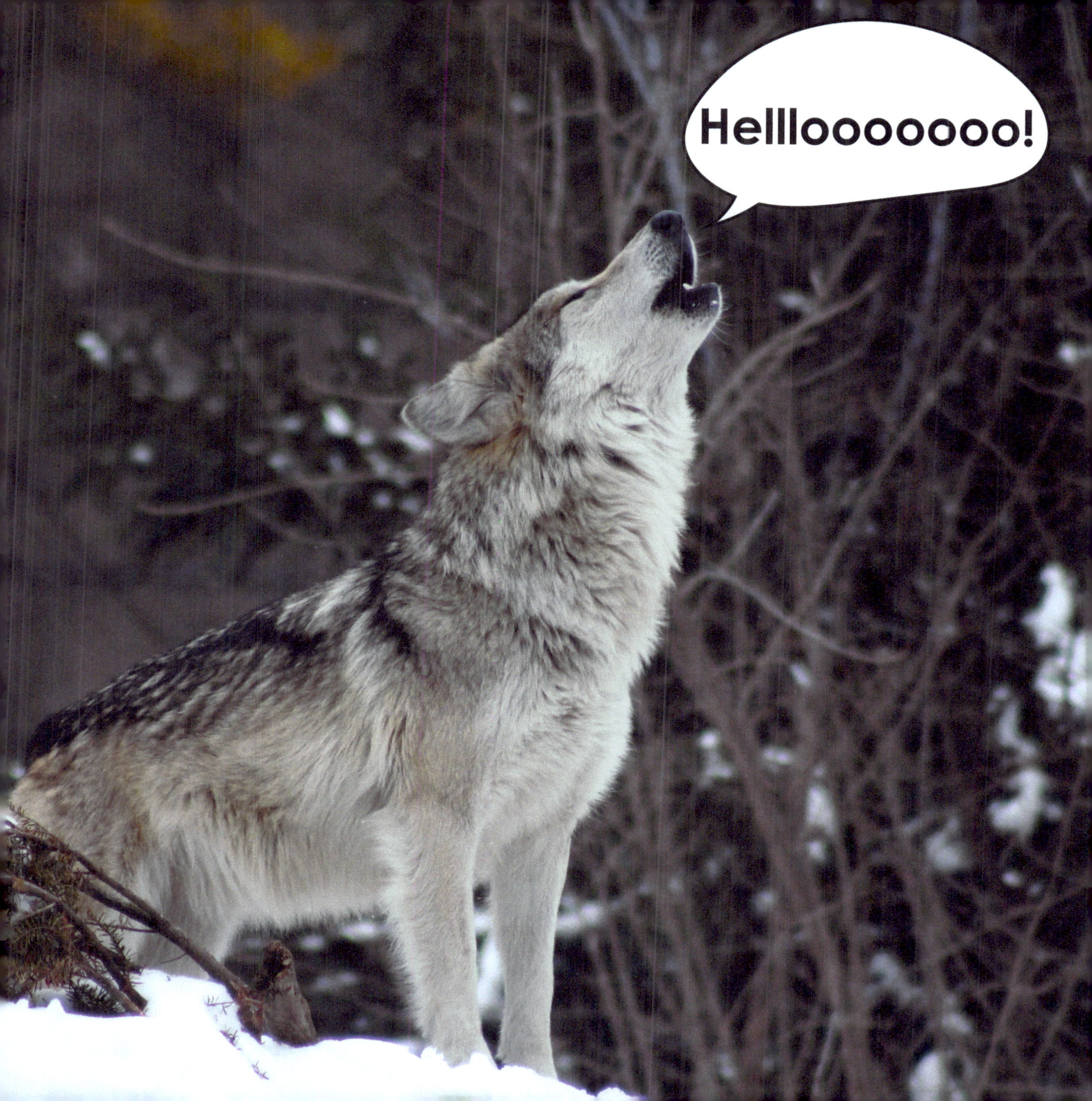
Hellloooooooo!

Each wolf has its own unique howl,
just like having its own special voice.

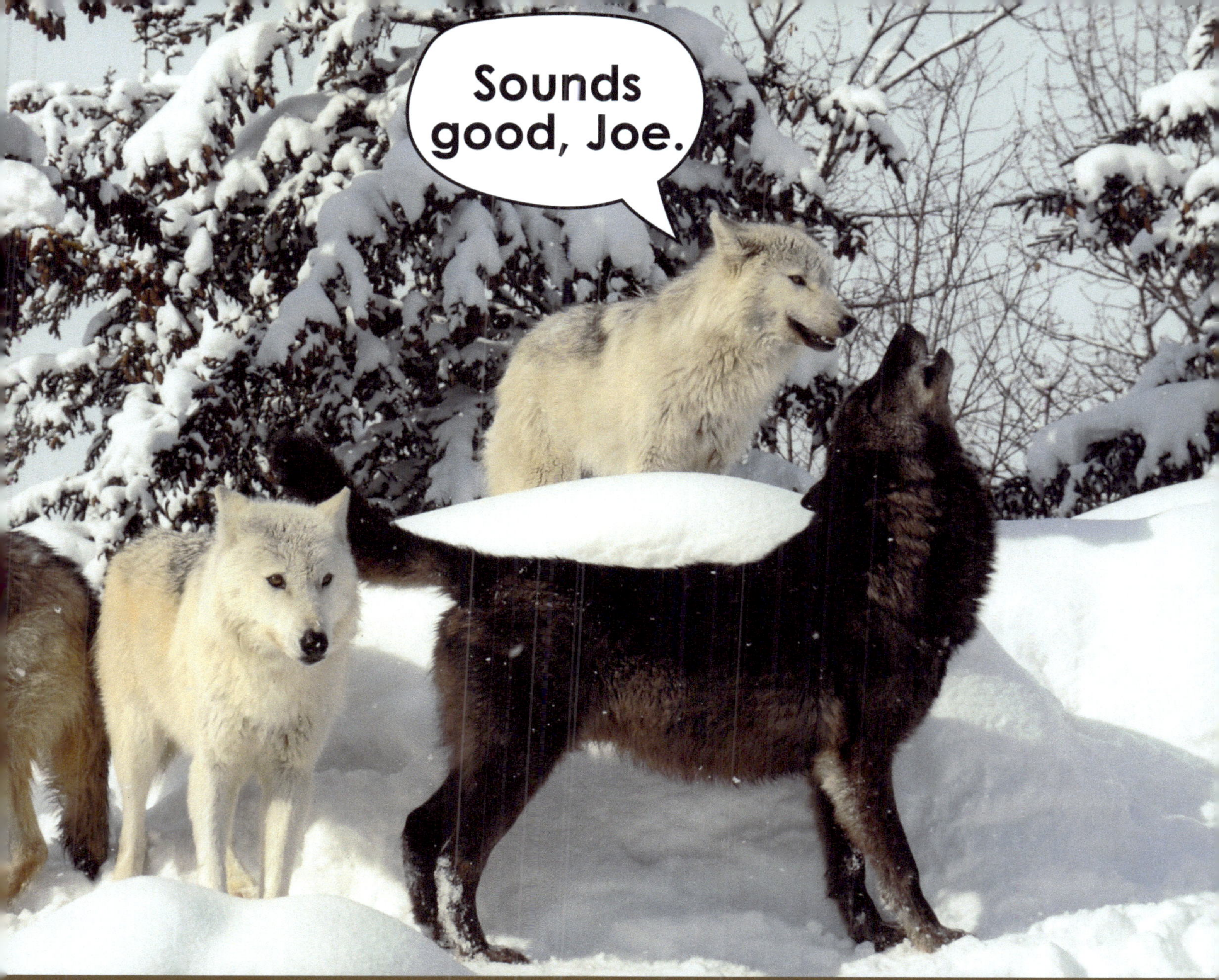

They can recognize who is who by their howls.

Wolves also use facial expressions to communicate feelings to other wolves.

Wolf pups are born blind and deaf. They have to rely on their parents and other pack members for care and protection.

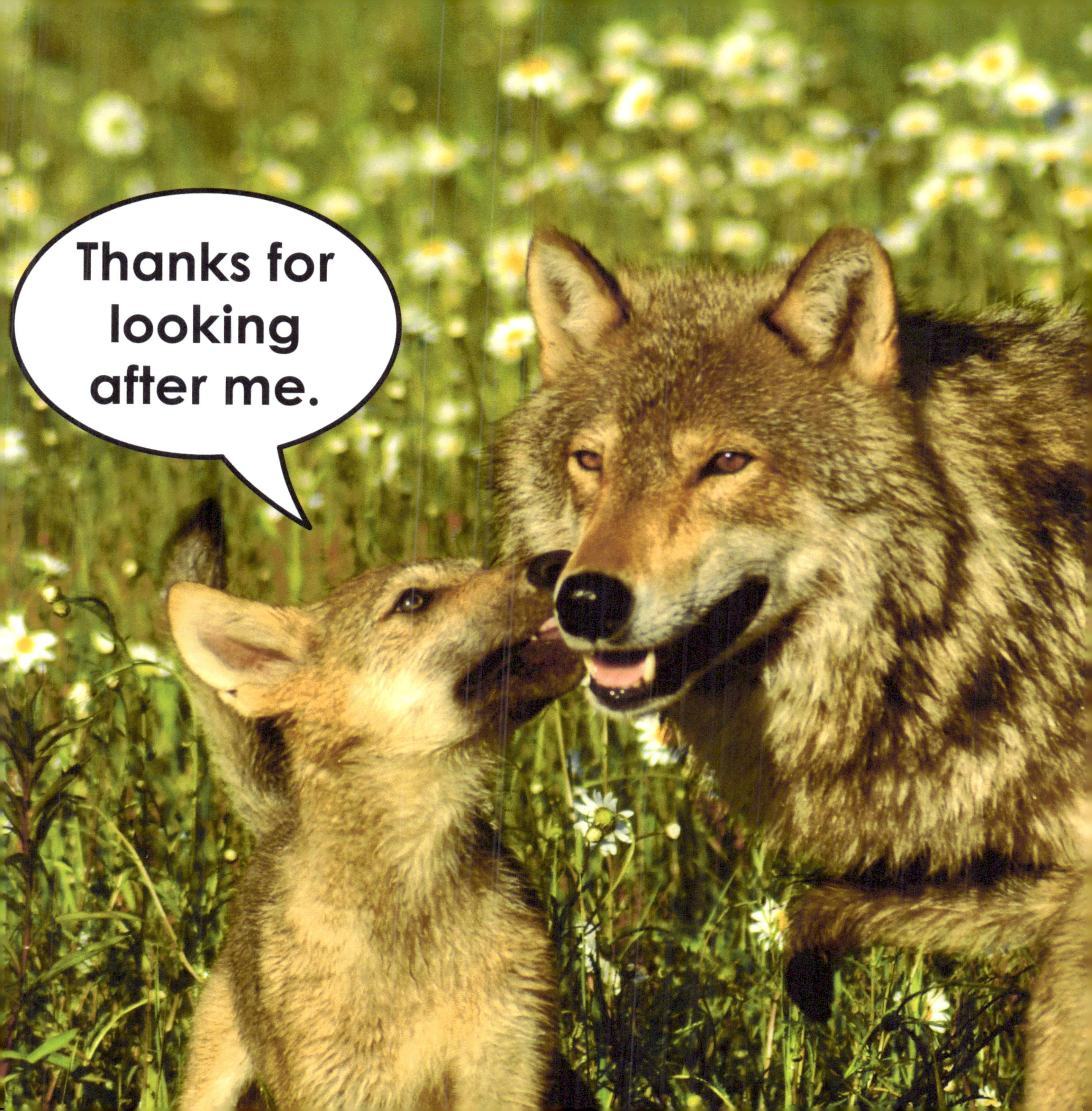
Thanks for looking after me.

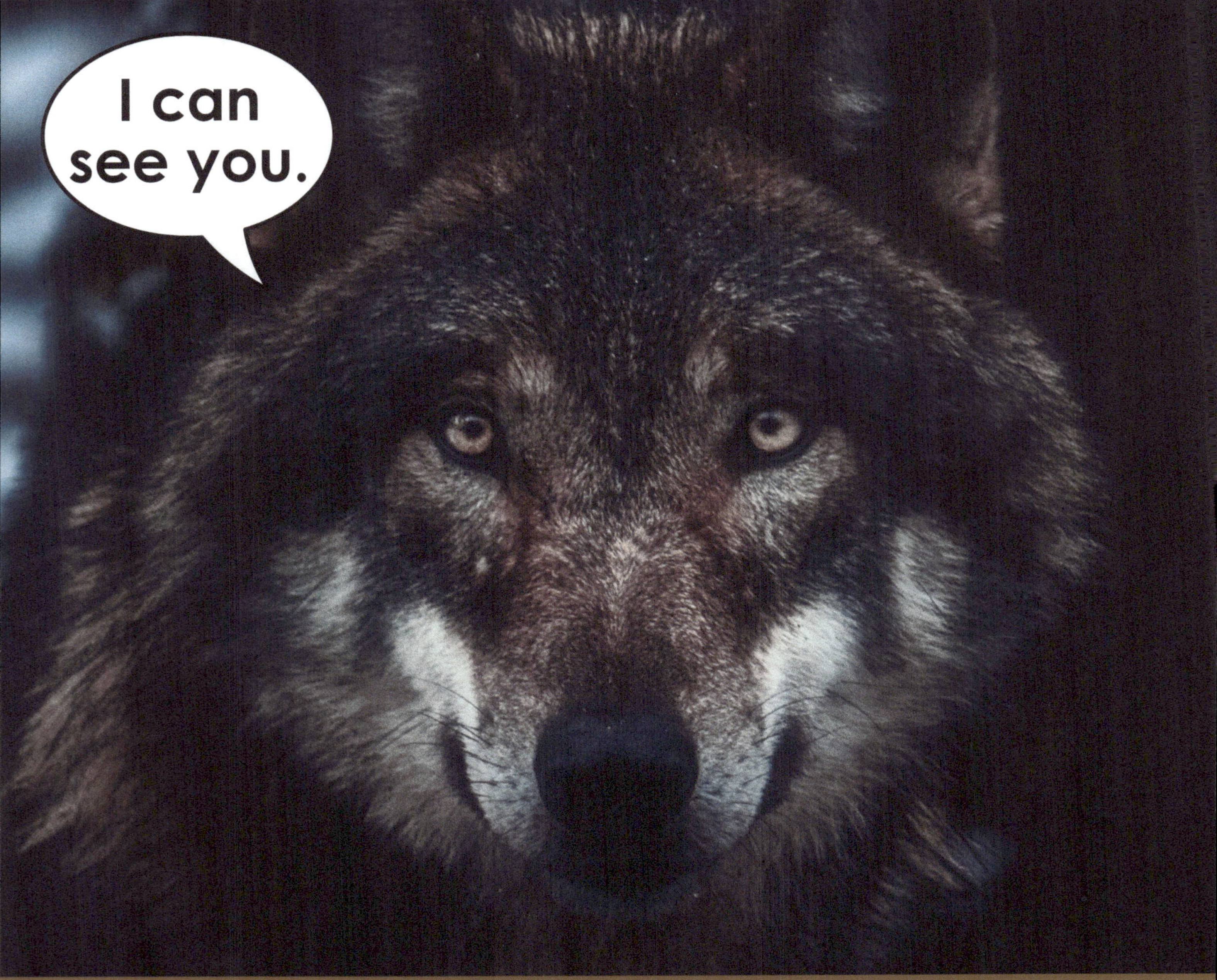

Wolves have excellent night vision.

But in the daytime their vision is not even as good as humans'.

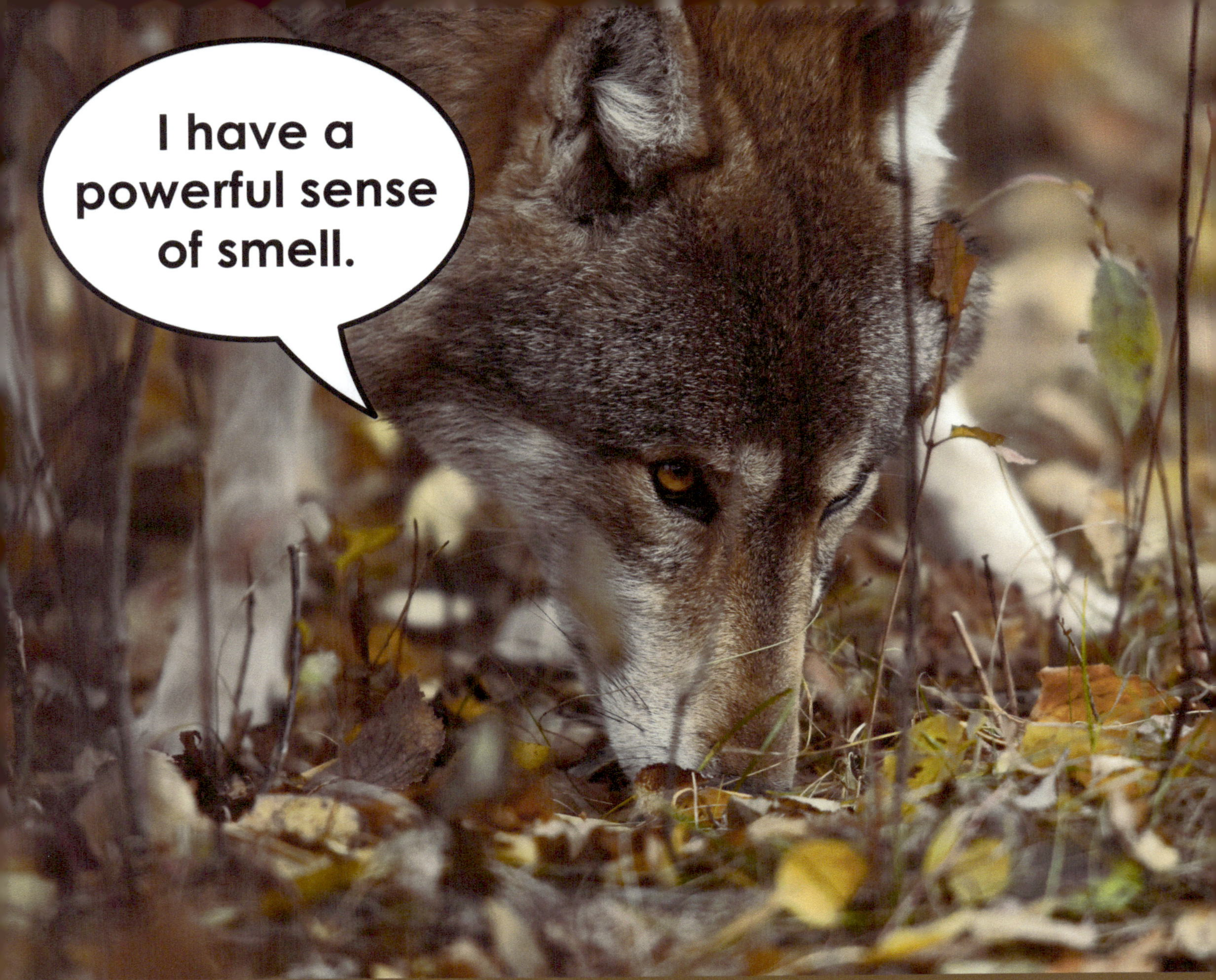

A wolf's nose helps them find prey when they hunt.

They can even smell things buried underground or hidden in the snow.

Wolves are patient hunters.
They observe their prey from far
away before making a move.

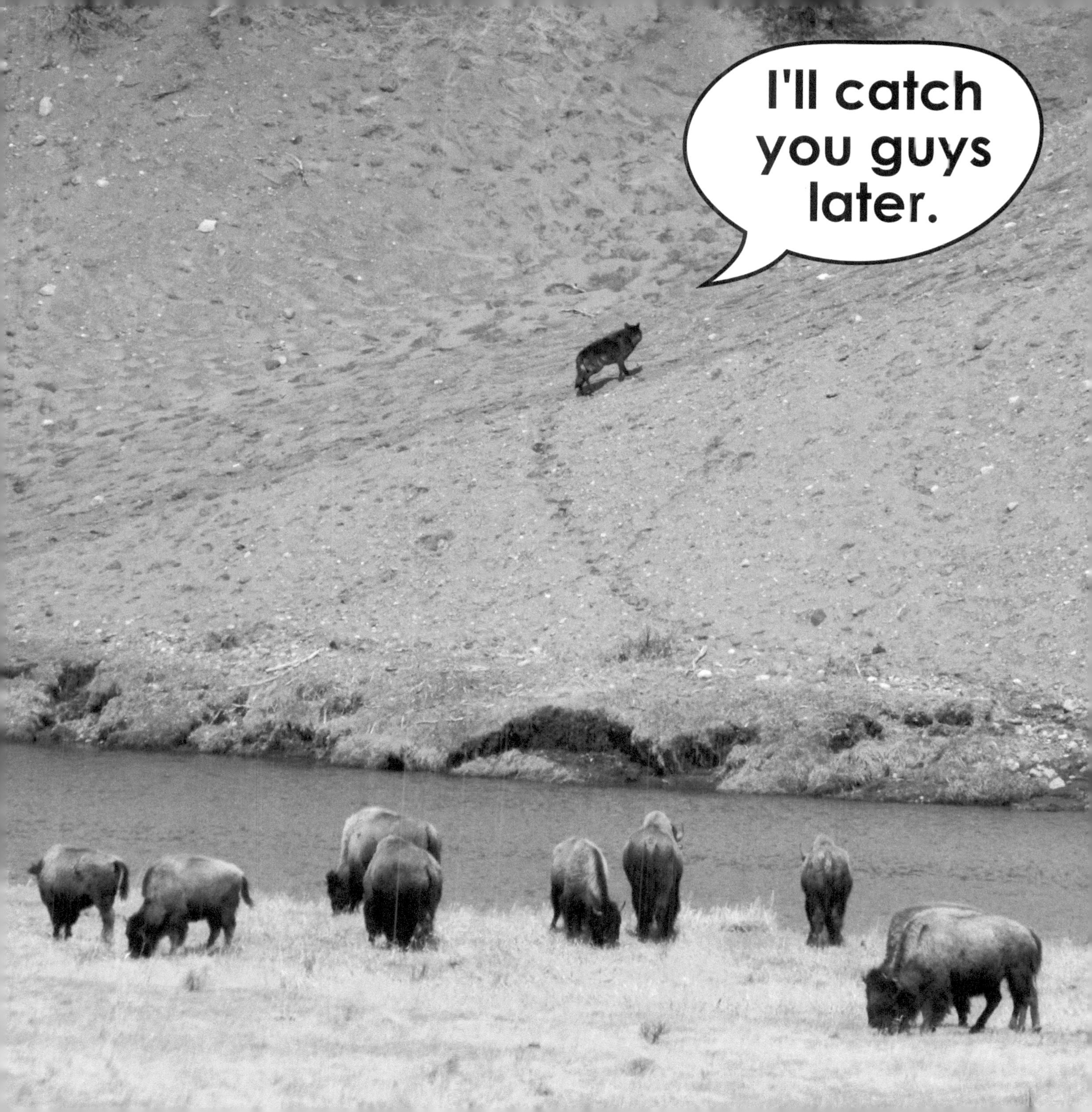
I'll catch you guys later.

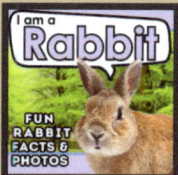

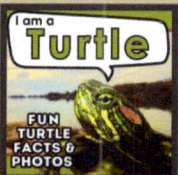

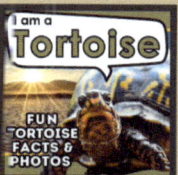

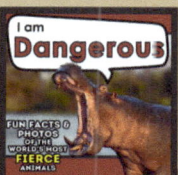

Hello parents!

scan here

Visit us to find out about new releases and *FREE* offers. We'll let you know when we have a new release coming out and how you can get it for FREE.
And you can cast your vote for what book we make next!

or visit here

ActiveBrainsBooks.com

scan here

Let us know what you think. As an independent publisher, your honest reviews mean a lot to us and our business. We'd love to hear from you!

amazon.com/review/create-review/

or visit here

FOLLOW US on Amazon.

amazon.com/author/activebrainsbooks

ActiveBrainsBooks.com

ACTIVE BRAINS